THE CALL
Youth Study Book

THE CALL
The Life and Message of the Apostle Paul

The Call
978-1-630-88262-4
978-1-630-88263-1 eBook

The Call: Large Print Edition
978-1-630-88264-8

The Call: DVD
978-1-630-88267-9

The Call: Leader Guide
978-1-630-88265-5
978-1-630-88266-2 eBook

The Call: Youth Study Book
978-1-630-88268-6
978-1-630-88269-3 eBook

The Call: Children's Leader Guide
978-1-630-88270-9

For more information, visit www.AdamHamilton.org.

Also by Adam Hamilton

24 Hours That Changed the World

Christianity and World Religions

Christianity's Family Tree

Confronting the Controversies

Enough

Final Words from the Cross

Forgiveness

Leading Beyond the Walls

Love to Stay

Making Sense of the Bible

Not a Silent Night

Revival

*Seeing Gray in a World of
   Black and White*

Selling Swimsuits in the Arctic

The Journey

The Way

Unleashing the Word

When Christians Get It Wrong

Why?

ADAM HAMILTON

THE CALL

THE LIFE AND MESSAGE OF
THE APOSTLE PAUL

YOUTH STUDY BOOK

by Mike Poteet

Abingdon Press / Nashville

THE CALL
THE LIFE AND MESSAGE OF THE APOSTLE PAUL

Youth Study Book
by Mike Poteet

This book is printed on elemental, chlorine-free paper.
ISBN 978-1-630-88268-6

15 16 17 18 19 20 21 22 23 24 — 10 9 8 7 6 5 4 3 2 1
MANUFACTURED IN THE UNITED STATES OF AMERICA

CONTENTS

INTRODUCTION

Apart from Jesus himself, the apostle Paul may be the most colorful, frequently controversial, and always intriguing figure in Christian history. He was perhaps the most widely traveled and certainly one of the most successful missionaries in the early church. The story of his journey from persecutor to preacher of "the Way" occupies most of the book of Acts. He is the undisputed author of at least eight letters in the New Testament (Romans, 1 and 2 Corinthians, Galatians, Philippians, 1 and 2 Thessalonians, and Philemon), and several more bear his name, although they may have been written by others representing his teachings (Ephesians, Colossians, 1 and 2 Timothy, and Titus). He has exercised an enormous influence on the church's theology and has commanded the attention and captured the imagination of generations of believers because of his bold proclamation of God's grace in Jesus.

But Paul didn't simply wake up one morning and decide to become one of the most famous men in religious and world history. He never saw himself as anyone but a faithful follower of Jesus. God called Paul to do some amazing things, but Paul was only expected to respond to God, as is any Christian. In this six-session exploration of Paul's life and work, we'll discover many dimensions of God's call to Paul, and think and talk about how they echo in God's call to each of us.

TO THE LEADER: USING THIS RESOURCE

In his book *The Call: The Life and Message of the Apostle Paul*, Adam Hamilton leads readers on a journey through Paul's work and writings, with special attention to Paul's missionary travels as recorded in the Acts of the Apostles. This youth study book complements *The Call*, using some of the same Scriptures and exploring several of the same themes through articles and activities appropriate for middle and high school youth. You may want to read *The Call* as part of your preparation to lead this study, but it is not required.

You will, however, want to provide each student in your group with a copy of this youth study book. Each chapter acts as a session plan you can use to chart your group's "itinerary" through Paul's life and ministry. The structure of each chapter and travel terminology of the chapters are shown here:

Point of Departure

Use these icebreaker questions and activities to get students talking, creating an atmosphere that will foster deeper study and discussion.

Scripture

Recruit one or more strong readers to read aloud the session's primary Scripture or Scriptures, or allow time for students to read the Scriptures on their own.

Video (Optional)

The Call includes six video presentations—one per chapter—which are available on DVD or by streaming. In these videos, Adam Hamilton leads viewers on a journey through Paul's life, showing places in which the apostle ministered and exploring how Paul's teaching helps us grow as Jesus' followers today. Consider introducing each of your group sessions with the corresponding video segment to help students visualize the context and appreciate the significance of Paul's work and words.

Getting Our Bearings

This section orients readers to important facts and themes in each chapter's study of Paul and his work and frequently develops themes from the material in ways relating to youth. Encourage students to read these articles on their own before each session (perhaps reminding them to do so via social media or e-mail). Rather than spending time reading this section during the session, read and review it yourself ahead of time and highlight main points.

Checkpoint Challenge

Each chapter includes a multiple-choice "trivia quiz" to help ensure that students grasp the session's factual content before they move on to interpretation and application. Some of the answers are joke answers. Answer keys are located at the end of each session (no peeking!).

Ports of Call

Each chapter suggests multiple activities designed to help students apply the biblical material to their lives. Use them all or choose based on time and interest. Some activities involve reading and discussion, while others involve planning projects that will require follow-up.

Postcard Prayer

As you close each session in a brief worship service, encourage students to respond to the prayer prompts on the "postcards to God" printed at the end of each chapter.

1.
CALLED TO FOLLOW CHRIST
PAUL'S BACKGROUND, CONVERSION, AND EARLY MINISTRY

Then [Paul] said: "I am a Jew, born in Tarsus in Cilicia, but brought up in [Jerusalem] at the feet of Gamaliel, educated strictly according to our ancestral law, being zealous for God, just as all of you are today. I persecuted this Way up to the point of death."

—Acts 22:2-4

Point of Departure

Choose two pieces at random from a jigsaw puzzle. On a blank sheet of paper, trace the puzzle pieces. Draw and doodle around the traced shapes to turn them into one of the following—or something entirely different!

- A remarkable new mode of mass transportation
- The first confirmed sighting of extraterrestrial life
- A caricature of a movie, TV, or music star
- A map of your hometown
- The prototype for a fantastic new piece of manufacturing machinery (be sure to describe what your contraption will make!)

Scripture

- Acts 9:1-29

Video (Optional)

- Watch the video for *The Call*, Session 1.

GETTING OUR BEARINGS

My grandmother Mimi loved solving jigsaw puzzles. She'd sit at her table for hours, sipping tea as she surveyed the brightly colored, weirdly shaped fragments of some unrecognizable image spread out in front of her. She'd sift this kaleidoscopic mess, looking back and forth between it and the picture printed on the puzzle's box. Every now and then she'd let loose a little cry of discovery—"Aha!" She'd snap a few pieces into place, nod her head in satisfaction, then lean back and look for more connections. Some she solved quicker than others, but she never met a jigsaw puzzle she couldn't master.

In *The Call*, Adam Hamilton says God used the "puzzle pieces" of the apostle Paul's life to "do something beautiful." Paul thought he knew how everything about him fit together. But like Mimi working those jigsaw puzzles, God patiently, persistently snapped Paul's "pieces" into place to reveal the picture they'd always been meant to show.

Bridging Two Worlds

Two important "puzzle pieces" framing Paul's life and work were his religious upbringing and social status.

Paul was a Jew. He was born into the tribe of Benjamin and was circumcised when eight days old, just as God's Law, the Torah, prescribes (Philippians 3:5). He learned to speak not only Greek, the common language of the Roman Empire, but also Hebrew, the language of Torah and one not every Jew in Paul's day still knew.[1] From an early age Paul studied Torah in Jerusalem, the Holy City itself, under Gamaliel (Acts 22:3), a rabbi (teacher) who was a high-ranking member of the Sanhedrin, the most important Jewish court. By birth and belief, Paul belonged to God's chosen people.

Paul was also a Roman citizen. In the mid- to late first century A.D., the Roman Empire was reaching the height of its power. Emperor Augustus (ruled 31 B.C.–A.D. 14) established a time of peace and prosperity called the *Pax Romana*, or "Roman peace," that would last over two centuries. The empire's network of roads—some fifty thousand miles of them, cutting straight, secure, water-repellent paths across varied terrain—ensured relatively easy movement of soldiers, commerce, and culture.

Most people who lived under Rome's authority were not imperial citizens, but Paul was privileged to be a citizen not only of his birthplace,

Tarsus (Acts 21:39), but also of the empire. As a citizen, Paul enjoyed more rights and fuller legal protection than noncitizens, including the right to vote, make contracts, avoid flogging, and appeal a case to the emperor.

Paul's background prepared him to bridge two worlds. Even his name points to his position: Hebrew speakers called him Saul, Greek speakers called him Paul, and he answered to either. He was always a Jew, as were Jesus and his disciples, and he used his Roman citizenship to gain the gospel a wider hearing.

Passion Repurposed

If Paul's life really were a jigsaw puzzle, it would be an exciting action scene—maybe even a 3-D image that "pops" when you view it through special glasses. Paul's life was full of excitement because Paul was passionate about faith.

Like his teacher Gamaliel, Paul was a Pharisee. Modern Christians tend to think poorly of Pharisees. We often assume they were mustache-twirling bad guys, because most Pharisees we read about in the Gospels are arguing with Jesus about how to understand Torah and plotting about putting him to death for his supposed blasphemy.

We forget those Pharisees didn't represent all Pharisees. In general, Pharisees were motivated by a desire to see *all* God's people, not just priests, living holy lives. Keeping the Law meant keeping the community's identity alive. In fact, when Rome destroyed the Jerusalem Temple in A.D. 70, the Pharisees' emphasis on every Jew's obligation to keep Torah helped Judaism survive.

Gamaliel was a reasonable, tolerant man (see his attitude toward Christians in Acts 5:33-39). Paul somehow missed that lesson! In his passion to protect Jewish faith from what he saw as misguided, dangerous ideas, he "persecuted this Way"—the Christian church's earliest name was the Way—"up to the point of death" (Acts 22:4). Luke, the Gospel writer who also wrote Acts, says Paul set out for the city of Damascus "breathing threats and murder against the disciples of the Lord" (Acts 9:1). Whenever I read that verse, I can't help picturing Paul as Darth Vader, breathing heavily as he sets out to crush a religious rebellion once and for all.

Had Hollywood dreamed up Paul's story, it might end with God smiting Paul dead—surely a fitting end for an enemy of the divine. The true story, however, is more unexpected and more wonderful. God smote him, all right, but with grace and a new beginning. The risen Jesus appeared to Paul on the road to Damascus and told him that Paul, who had spent so much energy and passion persecuting the Way, had been chosen to join it and had been given a key part to play in its growth.

Paul's conversion story is undeniably dramatic. It's *so* impressive, some Christians feel guilty if their own stories of coming to faith in Jesus don't pack the same spectacular punch. Paul, however, would be the last person to expect or demand that other Christians' "puzzles" look like his. As far as he was concerned, the *real* drama of his story was the joyful truth that God had given him new life, filled with new purpose—or, more accurately, a purpose new to Paul, but planned for him before he was born (Galatians 1:15).

The Son of Encouragement

Paul would also point out that the "puzzle" of his life doesn't picture him alone. His story is a story of people working together to do God's will—or of God working through them all.

One of Paul's earliest boosters was a man named Barnabas. His parents hadn't named him that; they called him Joseph. But he proved so generous in supporting the early church, the apostles gave him the name, which means "Son of Encouragement" (Acts 4:36-37).

Barnabas's encouragement made a big difference to Paul. When Paul, early persecutor of the Way, tried to join Jesus' disciples in Jerusalem, he didn't find any red carpet rolled out for him. Only when Barnabas vouched for Paul did church leaders give him their "thumbs up" (see Acts 9:26-28).

Even then, Paul's missionary career didn't take off. His preaching led to some heated arguments; his opponents got so angry they tried to kill him! The Jerusalem church helped Paul make a getaway back to Tarsus. Paul might have wondered when God's big plans for his future would kick in.

When they did, Barnabas was involved. News reached Jerusalem that many Jews and non-Jews were joining the Way in Antioch in Syria, the third biggest city in the Roman Empire. Church leaders sent Barnabas to investigate this development. He checked out the situation and reached the only possible conclusion: God's grace was at work! And he concluded something else: Paul would be a perfect fit for it. Barnabas brought Paul back from Tarsus, and for the next year "they met with the church and taught a great many people"—

so many that the Way started to become recognized as something distinct from Judaism: in Antioch, "the disciples were first called 'Christians'" (Acts 11:26).

Who has encouraged you? Who has glimpsed ways you might use your experience, education, skills and talents, and unique perspective to answer God's call? When I was a teenager, I spent hours scribbling stories and plays. The stuff wasn't Shakespeare, but my Aunt Cora took an interest in it. She would ask about my plots and characters; she encouraged me to keep thinking and writing; she gave me a personalized three-ring binder in which to file my literary creations. Today, writing is an important part of how I serve the church. I'm sure Cora's encouragement is a big reason why.

God might be calling you to encourage someone. We're not always the best judge of what we can do, or what we have to offer. We often need others to point out possibilities we haven't considered, directions we haven't explored. Do you see ways your friends, classmates, or people in your congregation and community might be a perfect fit for something "the hand of the Lord" (Acts 11:21) is doing?

Many Solutions—One Solver

Jigsaw puzzles have a single solution. But God can fit the pieces of our lives together into more than one beautiful picture. Even Paul's response to God took a number of shapes and contained several surprising twists. Maybe a life pieced together by God is most like a puzzle printed with a lenticular image—the finished picture moves and shifts depending on the angle and the light.

We can respond to God's claim and call in many different faithful ways. What does stay the same is God's presence with and love for us. Paul believed nothing can separate us from God's love in Jesus Christ (Romans 8:38-39). He'd experienced that truth in his own story. If this ever-faithful God pieced together the life of Paul, who'd persecuted the church, into a beautiful picture, then God can master the pieces that make up your life and mine.

CHECKPOINT CHALLENGE

1. Identify and correct any statements about Paul below that are not true.
   a. He belonged to the tribe of Benjamin.
   b. He spoke Greek, Hebrew, and Babylonian.
   c. He was a Roman citizen.
   d. He studied Torah in Nazareth.

2. Paul was on his way to what city when the risen Jesus appeared to him?
   a. Jerusalem
   b. Damascus
   c. Tarsus
   d. Antioch
   e. New York, New York

3. Who laid hands on Paul to restore his sight to him?
   a. Ananias
   b. John Mark
   c. Barnabas
   d. Gamaliel

4. The name of Paul's early supporter Barnabas means what?
   a. Son of Discernment
   b. Son of Wisdom
   c. Son of Encouragement
   d. Son of Righteousness
   e. Son of Krypton

5. Which of the following are two things Barnabas did to support Paul?
   a. He baptized Paul and instructed him in the teachings of Jesus.
   b. He recommended him to church leaders in Jerusalem.
   c. He helped him escape his opponents in Damascus.
   d. He recruited Paul for missionary work in Antioch.

PORTS OF CALL

Pauline Play

The story of Paul's conversion practically demands to be dramatized! Recruit someone to read aloud Acts 9:1-22 and people to pantomime the roles of Paul (Saul), his companions, Ananias, the disciples in Damascus, and worshipers in the synagogues. Be certain to record your performance so others in your congregation can watch it. (If your congregation or youth ministry has a website, see if the performance can be posted there, too.) After the show, respond to these questions:

- How does this dramatization affect the way I think about Paul's conversion?
- With which character—Paul, Ananias, or an amazed onlooker—do I most identify, and why?
- What specific response to God do I hope audiences of this performance will make?

Internet Option: Search for others' dramatizations of Paul's conversions on YouTube or other video site, and reflect on several of those dramatizations using the same questions.

Tell Your Story

Read Acts 22:1-16. Whether or not the story of your faith in Jesus is as dramatic as Paul's, it's a story worth telling! So practice telling your story—your testimony to how God brought you to believe in Jesus Christ. Your testimony won't be exactly like Paul's, but you can think about some elements in his story to help you tell yours. Prayerfully consider these questions:

- How have the places you've lived helped shape who you are or pre-pared you for faith, as Tarsus helped shape Paul?
- What individuals have taught you about God and Scripture, as Gamaliel and Ananias taught Paul?
- When have you "seen the light"—not necessarily a blinding flash, as Paul did, but some sign, small or large, of God's presence with and care for you?

- In what ways have you changed for the better over your life, as Paul changed? Were these gradual or sudden changes? How might God have been guiding you in these changes?
- What skills and gifts do you possess that you use in serving Jesus, as Paul used his skills and gifts?

You may not have answers to all these questions right now. That's okay. Paul had a lifetime to refine his testimony. If you have even a sentence or two about the difference Jesus makes in your life, you already have a testimony to tell. Practice telling it to another Christian, and let that person practice as you listen. The more comfortable you are in telling your story inside the community of faith, the more prepared you'll be to tell it outside, where your story may be just the story through which someone hears God's call to them too.

Puzzle Pieces

On a blank sheet of white cardstock or posterboard, draw pictures (or paste images from magazines and newspapers) to represent at least two of the following: your family background; your skills and abilities; at least one past experience you consider personally significant; someone else who is important to you. Cut this collage into several small, jigsaw-like puzzle pieces. Trade puzzles with someone else. When you and your partner have solved both puzzles, take turns interviewing each other about the images in them. Be sure to ask each other:

- What purposes do you think God might see in the "pieces" of your life?

Tarsus Treat

Remember Paul's home of Tarsus by making and enjoying lahmacun (la-ma-ZHUN), a popular food from southern Turkey. You can find easy-to-follow recipes online. As you prepare the food, discuss:

- How did God prepare Paul for his service as an apostle?
- For what service might God be preparing you today?

Be Like Barnabas

Barnabas demonstrated two important qualities of Christians: encouragement and generosity. Follow his example by doing one or both of the following:

- Write a note or make a card of encouragement and send it to someone you think would appreciate an encouraging word. Consider not only people who might be feeling down but also people in whom you see experience or talents that God could use for good, as Barnabas saw such qualities in Paul.
- With others in your youth ministry or congregation, sell some of your possessions and donate the money you raise to your church, as Barnabas sold a field to help fund the apostles' ministry.

Puzzle Picture Frame

If you have an old jigsaw puzzle that's missing pieces, recycle it by turning it into a picture frame. Take a picture of yourself that you like and glue it to a backing of corrugated cardboard. Glue jigsaw puzzle pieces around the picture's edge, building up two or three layers. Glue a length of yarn to the picture backing to hang it on a wall.

POSTCARD PRAYER

[Leader: Have participants write responses in the "postcard" printed below, or provide actual postcards they can present in worship as an offering to God.]

Dear God, thank you especially for this piece of my life:

_____

_____

_____

_____

_____

Checkpoint Challenge Answer Key: 1.b (not Babylonian); d (Jerusalem, not Nazareth); 2.b; 3.a; 4.c; 5.b and d

2.
CALLED TO GO
PAUL'S FIRST MISSIONARY JOURNEY

While they were worshiping the Lord and fasting, the Holy Spirit said, "Set apart for me Barnabas and Saul for the work to which I have called them."

—Acts 13:2

Point of Departure

Option A. On a United States or world map, mark the states or countries where you've been with your initials. Compare your travels to others in your group. Who's been the farthest? Who's been to the most unusual destination? Among all of you, how many miles has your group traveled?

Option B. On a separate sheet of paper, design a brochure that describes and pictures the "trip of a lifetime" that you'd love to take. Where would you go? What would you see? Who would go with you? Money and time are no object, so dream big!

Scriptures

- Acts 13:13-52
- Romans 10:5-17

Video (Optional)

- Watch the video for *The Call*, Session 2.

GETTING OUR BEARINGS

Everybody's had times when they've embarrassed themselves so badly, they want nothing more than to curl up in a tiny ball and hide. One of those moments hit me when I was in an interfaith student group in college. I was asked to begin a meeting with a prayer. I thanked God for bringing us together from different backgrounds to serve our campus and community and asked God to bless our discussion and our planning. And when it was time to end my prayer, I said—without a moment's thought—"In Jesus' name. Amen."

It felt like the air in the room turned to ice. I had to stop myself from reaching out to try and pull back the words as they dropped from my lips like a lead weight. I was mortified, and hurriedly said, "Oh, I'm so sorry." But it was too late. Our group's leader, a young Jewish woman, had visibly tensed—her back stiff, her hands gripping her chair's arms. "That's all right," she muttered, not very convincingly, avoiding my eyes.

It wasn't that I was ashamed to be Christian. What upset me was knowing I'd caused offense by unthinkingly invoking Jesus. Had I been praying as attentively as I should have, I could have spoken words that were both true to my own faith and inclusive of others, especially our group's Jewish members. In that instant, I'd been insensitive and ungracious literally in Jesus' name.

Jesus of Nazareth was a devout Jew. So were all his first followers. So how and why did the Way—the movement of Jews who believed Jesus was the Messiah who had been promised to God's chosen people, Israel—end up parting ways with Judaism? How did Jesus' name, praised by some Jews, come to be hurtful, even hateful, to others?

The First Missionary Journey

We can spot the split between Judaism and Christianity taking shape in what Bible readers have long called Paul's "first missionary journey." Paul had already taken more than one trip to preach about Jesus, but was now taking the gospel into unfamiliar territory.

And so the Spirit led Paul and Barnabas to the island of Cyprus, about 250 miles northwest of Jerusalem (Acts 13:4). They then went to the mainland of what is today Turkey: first to the city of Perga (13:13), and then to Antioch of Pisidia (13:14—not Antioch in Syria, where Jesus' followers were first called

Christians). Their itinerary included stops in Iconium (14:1) and the region in and around Lystra and Derbe (14:6). Finally, the apostles backtracked their route (14:21-25) and sailed to Antioch (of Syria, this time), where they reported back to the church. In *The Call*, Adam Hamilton estimates this first missionary journey covered some 1,580 miles and lasted between six months and a year.

What could make you travel that far or that long? Thanks to cars and planes, great distances don't necessarily challenge us as they did Paul and Barnabas. But could you uproot yourself for months at a time? *Would* you, even if you could? Currently, the average length of an American vacation is 3.8 days.[2] If we don't manage to take even a full four days for vacation, how many days would we be likely to take for the kind of physically and spiritually demanding trip Paul took?

Some of you may someday spend a semester or more studying abroad—and if you're fortunate enough to have that opportunity, take it—but that travel benefits you. Paul spent months and years abroad for others' benefit.

Some of you have gone or will go on church-sponsored mission trips—and, again, if you can, do so; you'll likely forge strong friendships, do good work, and quite possibly enlarge your outlook on life. Paul's mission trips, however, weren't carefully planned, short-term, or generally safe affairs. Check out 2 Corinthians 11:23-28. If your youth group's leader handed you a mission trip brochure that read like *that*, would you still sign up?

Missionary M.O.

Paul signed up, and more than once. Each trip he took proved unique, but they all followed a pattern set in that first journey—a *modus operandi* (or "m.o." as TV detectives say), a well-established way of doing things. Once he reached his destination, Paul would visit a local synagogue (Jewish house of worship), pray and listen to Scripture with the congregation, and then preach a sermon in which he announced "that what God promised to our ancestors he has fulfilled for us...by raising Jesus" from death (Acts 13:32-33).

Note that Paul didn't *start* by talking about the first Easter. He would review the history of God's relationship with Israel. God chose Abraham to father a family in whom all the world's families would find blessing. God rescued Abraham's descendants from slavery in Egypt. God led them to the Promised Land, ultimately choosing David to rule as their earthly king. All of Paul's hearers could recite this story along with him. Only then did Paul declare that "God has brought to Israel a Savior, Jesus" from David's posterity, as promised (Acts 13:23).

Paul wasn't trying to pull a fast one. His sermon was no bait-and-switch, but was backstory necessary for making sense of Jesus. As Paul would later write, "from them"—meaning the Jewish people, to whom he belonged— "comes the Messiah" (Romans 9:5). Jesus himself states, in John's Gospel, that "salvation is from the Jews" (John 4:22). It only makes sense, then, that Paul would, wherever he went, tell Jews first about what God had done in Jesus' death and resurrection: "by this Jesus everyone who believes is set free from all those sins from which you could not be freed by the law of Moses" (Acts 13:39). For Paul, Jesus was reason for his fellow Jews to rejoice!

But they didn't. They didn't in Antioch or Iconium, and most Jews don't now. Just today I watched a Jewish comedian on TV good-naturedly say, "We Jews embrace Jesus as one of our own—to a certain point." The joke got a big laugh; I laughed, too. But the fact that not all Jews embraced Jesus as the Christ was no laughing matter for Paul. "If there was any way I could be cursed by the Messiah so they could be blessed by him," Paul would later write, "I'd do it in a minute" (Romans 9:3 *THE MESSAGE*). Instead, when he and his message met with opposition, all Paul could do was follow Jesus' own instructions to shake that place's dust off his feet and move on (see Luke 9:5).

In Antioch, Paul and Barnabas told their fellow Jews "it was necessary" to hear the message about Jesus first. That phrase implies more than practical necessity; it points to God's will. But Paul and Barnabas continued, "Since you reject it and judge yourselves to be unworthy of eternal life, we are now turning to the Gentiles. For so the Lord has commanded us..." (Acts 13:46-47).

Beautiful Feet, Faithful Friendships

Paul's obedient move toward non-Jews accelerated the church's transformation into a movement that cut across all sorts of boundaries. Unfortunately, it also created divisions that have caused plenty of pain.

Paul's talk of Jews "judging themselves unworthy of eternal life" is harsh, and reflects the raw emotion in the early days of the church's split from the synagogue. It also sounds at odds with Paul's own insistence on the importance of God's grace: *no one* is worthy of eternal life, though we receive it (see Romans 3:23-24). Belief in Jesus as the Messiah may seem obvious to us; two millennia of church history have trained us to read the Old Testament as testimony to him. We're not wrong, but we read the Hebrew Scriptures trusting Jesus to show himself there. Jesus' identity as the Savior isn't self-evident. It's not an ironclad mathematical proof or some scientific result that can be replicated in a lab. To say Jesus is the Messiah, the Christ, is to say that we trust, despite sometimes conflicting evidence, that Jesus is who he tells us he is, and who we've experienced hm to be. Paul knew such faith only comes as God's gift.

Does that mean we shouldn't continue to proclaim Jesus as Messiah? As Paul frequently says in his letters, "By no means!" (The Greek phrase really means something along the lines of, "Heck, no!") Paul references the prophet Isaiah: "How beautiful are the feet of those who bring good news!" (Romans 10:15; see Isaiah 52:7). If you've been baptized as a Christian, if you've been confirmed as a follower of Jesus Christ, then—no matter how you think they look (or smell)—your feet are beautiful! God has given you the responsibility and privilege of taking the gospel to other people. You'll encounter plenty of people to whom you can proclaim the gospel wherever your feet take you, around the world or around the corner.

Your missionary "m.o." may not look like Paul's. Instead of marching into a synagogue to preach, you might start with friends who aren't believers. Don't be preachy, but patient. Listen to their concerns and struggles— if you're really their friend, you already do. Focus on being the best friend you can be. Look for opportunities that naturally present themselves to speak simple, humble words about the difference Jesus makes to you. Don't assume you know how Jesus will be active in your friends' lives, only trust that he will (and, indeed, already is). And remember that what you do and how you act will ultimately speak the gospel louder than any words you say.

CHECKPOINT CHALLENGE

1. Most of the destinations in Paul's first missionary journey were located where?
   a. Egypt
   b. Modern-day Turkey
   c. Modern-day Syria
   d. Italy

2. Which of the following statements best describes Paul's standard procedure during his missionary travels?
   a. He would visit only local synagogues.
   b. He would preach to local non-Jews before visiting synagogues.
   c. He would visit local synagogues before preaching to non-Jews.
   d. He would preach in local marketplaces to anyone who would listen.

3. Which of the following statements is *not* something Paul believed about his fellow Jews?
   a. Jesus fulfilled all God's promises to Israel.
   b. He wished he could be cursed if it would mean more of them would accept Jesus as Messiah.
   c. The fact that more of them did not accept Jesus as Messiah meant God's promises had failed.
   d. God willed that Jews should hear the message of salvation through Jesus before Gentiles.

4. What did Paul and Barnabas do in Antioch of Pisidia to protest those who did not accept the gospel?
   a. They tore their clothes in an ancient expression of grief.
   b. They shook the dust of the place from their feet.
   c. They put on sackcloth and ashes and prayed for those who had rejected their preaching.
   d. They prayed God would destroy the town with fire from heaven.

5. Whose feet did Paul, referencing Isaiah, say are beautiful?
   a. The feet with which Jesus walked the earth.
   b. The feet of those who bring good news.
   c. The feet of those who hunger and thirst for righteousness.
   d. The feet of those who worship God in spirit and truth.

PORTS OF CALL

Salvation History Mural

In Antioch of Pisidia, as wherever he preached to his fellow Jews, Paul always took care to show how Jesus fit into Israel's salvation history—its past experiences of God's saving and sustaining power. On a long sheet of brown or white paper, illustrate the highlights of salvation history that Paul pointed to in his sermon in Acts 13:

- the Exodus from Egypt (v. 17)
- wandering in the wilderness (v. 18)
- conquest of Canaan, the Promised Land (v. 19)
- the era of the judges (v. 20)
- King Saul (v. 21)
- King David (v. 22)
- John the Baptist (vv. 23-25)

Since Paul didn't describe these events and people in great detail, you may need to work with a Bible dictionary or concordance for ideas about illustrating them. (Option: find and piece together appropriate illustrations from old Sunday school materials or online sources.) End your mural with an illustration of Jesus' death and resurrection (Acts 13:27-33). As you work with others on the mural, discuss these questions:

- Why did Paul choose to include these particular people and events in his preaching about Jesus?
- How would you answer someone who said to you, "Why should Christians bother reading the Old Testament? There's nothing about Jesus in there."?
- How are we encouraged today by Paul's teaching about how Jesus answers God's promises to Israel?

The Word Is Near

Romans 10:5-17 presents the difference Paul sees between two ways of trying to have "righteousness," or a right relationship with God. One is the impossible task of trying to earn it by keeping God's law perfectly. The other is receiving the right relationship that God freely gives through faith in Jesus

Christ. Paul stresses that we don't have to go to impossible lengths to find righteousness, because the word of faith is near us.

Make a necklace or wristlet to remind yourself "the word is near." String letter beads on a length of plastic or leather cord (check with local craft or art supply stores) to spell out a word or phrase that will encourage you in your faith. (If you don't want to wear your creation, hang it on your bedroom doorknob, on the car's rearview mirror, or someplace else where you will frequently see it.) As you work with others on this craft, discuss these questions:

- How are both what we say and what we believe important in our salvation?
- Do verses 9-10 contradict Paul's insistence that nothing we can do will make us right with God? Why or why not?
- If keeping God's law wasn't intended to make us righteous, why did God give the law—and should Christians worry about keeping it today?

Your Beautiful Feet!

Trace one of your feet on a piece of construction paper. Cut out the tracing. Write or draw on it about one specific way you will bring the good news of God's love in Jesus to someone else this week. Decorate your "foot" in any additional ways you choose, then keep it someplace where you'll see it frequently—on your bedroom wall, in your school locker—as a reminder that God calls you to help others hear the gospel.

Meet a Missionary

If someone in your congregation has served as a missionary, invite that person to speak with your group during your study of *The Call.* (Your pastor or another church leader may be able to help you identify someone to invite.) Ask such questions as:

- How did you hear God's call to mission work?
- Where did you serve, and how did you go about spreading the gospel?
- How did you experience God at work in your mission?
- What can we do to support missionaries who are still working in the field?

If you cannot invite a missionary speaker, learn about missionaries your congregation is currently supporting, either directly or through a missionary organization. If possible, write and send notes of remembrance and encouragement to one or more of these missionaries. Tell them something you have learned about mission from your study of the apostle Paul.

Sing a Spiritual

Sing or recite together the hymn "Guide My Feet." You can find the lyrics and melody online. Improvise your own additional verses (for example, "Use my gifts...." "Keep me brave...." "Show me hope...").

POSTCARD PRAYER

[Leader: Have participants write responses in the "postcard" printed below, or provide actual postcards they can present in worship as an offering to God.]

Dear God, help me point to Jesus in all my friendships, and especially with these people:

_____

_____

_____

_____

_____

Checkpoint Challenge Answer Key: 1.b; 2.c; 3.c; 4.b; 5.b

3.
CALLED TO SUFFER
PAUL'S SECOND MISSIONARY JOURNEY (1)

During the night Paul had a vision: there stood a man of Macedonia
pleading with him and saying, "Come over to Macedonia and help us."
                                                                    —Acts 16:9

Point of Departure

On a separate sheet of paper, sketch each of the danger signs described
(answers are at the end of the session).

  a. a symbol that means "Don't eat or drink this!"
  b. an indication on old maps of unknown perils in uncharted waters
  c. a traffic sign indicating the need to slow down

Scriptures

  • Acts 15:36-41
  • Acts 16:16-40

Video (Optional)

  • Watch the video for *The Call*, Session 3.

GETTING OUR BEARINGS

Monty Python and the Holy Grail is one of the funniest films ever made.
It's hard to single out any of its many great bits as the best, but "The Tale
of Brave Sir Robin" comes close. When this supposedly bold Knight of the

Round Table decides things are getting too adventurous, he makes a quick exit, to the painfully honest, thoroughly hysterical accompaniment of a merry minstrel: "Brave, brave Sir Robin, he bravely ran away…When danger reared its ugly head, he bravely turned his tail and fled; brave Sir Robin turned about and gallantly he chickened out…"

The apostle Paul was no Sir Robin! Beatings, jail time, shipwrecks—Paul faced all these troubles and more without flinching (2 Corinthians 11:23-29). But he was no adrenaline junkie, seeking danger for danger's sake. He wrote: "I'm all right with weaknesses, insults, disasters, harassments, and stressful situations for the sake of Christ" (2 Corinthians 12:10 CEB).

During his second missionary journey, Paul suffered through several kinds of conflict. Like Jesus' first disciples, however, he regarded suffering for the sake of Jesus as a privilege (Acts 5:41). He believed the conflicts he faced confirmed that he was faithfully following the Savior.

Conflict with Others

Paul and Barnabas worked well together during their first missionary journey. Sending them out again to check on the congregations they'd left behind must have seemed a sure thing. But no sooner had they started planning their itinerary than they were arguing. Barnabas wanted once again to bring his cousin, John Mark, but Paul wasn't so eager. John didn't finish the first missionary trip. Luke doesn't tell us why (Acts 13:13), only that Paul thought John deserted them. Unable to agree, Paul and Barnabas chose separate companions—Barnabas took John while Paul took Silas (called Silvanus in Paul's letters)—and went their separate ways.

Was Paul in the right? Or was this argument another example of the temper and stubbornness we sometimes see flare up in Paul's letters? We don't know. All we know is Paul believed the integrity of his mission mattered more than his friendship with Barnabas—the same man who'd defended him to the Jerusalem leaders, who had brought him from Tarsus to begin his work for the Lord. Paul owed Barnabas much but felt that he owed God more. Again, we're not told that God weighed in on the team's lineup. Paul may have been relying simply on his own best judgment. But Jesus' followers must sometimes do just that, even if it causes conflict.

When Christians fight about how best to follow Jesus—and, as much as we'd like to think otherwise, we do—we must avoid the temptation to decide too quickly that we're right. Sincere as our beliefs may be, others believe just as sincerely. This fact doesn't mean everyone is right, but it does mean we must listen lovingly and prayerfully to sisters and brothers in Christ with whom we disagree. God might be saying something through them that we need to hear.

And when following Jesus creates conflict with non-Christians, we have to be especially careful. Maybe you've run up against many nonbelievers' images of Christians: sour-faced, tongue-clucking, finger-wagging goody-goodies who think they're better than everyone. As a follower of Jesus, you will find yourself in situations where you can't just go with the crowd. But it's often possible to go against the crowd gracefully—to do the right thing quietly, without calling attention to yourself, or to keep the focus on Jesus, where it belongs.

Luke didn't say whether Paul and Barnabas tried to work out their differences. Whatever else happened, their sharp disagreement shows us that saying yes to God sometimes means saying no to other people—even fellow believers, even friends.

Conflict with Evil

Are evil spirits real? In a recent survey, 57 percent of respondents said they think demons exist and can possess people.[3] Stories in the Bible, such as the apostles' encounter with the slave girl in Philippi, certainly show para-normal forces at work. The spirit who gave this girl an apparent ability to read fortunes and tell futures wasn't directly called *evil*, but considering Scripture's negative view of magic and the occult, it's probably not some friendly ghost.

This spirit's outbursts resembled times when demons recognized and announced Jesus as God's Holy One, before he silenced and sent them away (for example, Luke 4:33-36; 8:26-39). Those incidents, like this one, indicate that the spread of the gospel has cosmic consequences. Whenever the Word of God shows up—whether in the flesh, in Jesus, or through the words and actions of his followers—evil sounds the alarm. As the apostle James wrote, "Even the demons believe—and shudder" (James 2:19). The spirit enslaving this young woman knew that Paul and his companions were slaves of a greater Master, bringing good news of salvation and freedom. No wonder the spirit shouted: the gospel was a threat to it! The reality of evil is a given for Christian faith. Whatever you may decide about demons, there's no denying dark forces really do threaten and destroy human life.

Greed is one of those forces. Greed, in fact, is the real demon in this story. I don't know if this girl could really tell people's fortunes; she may have been using the kinds of tricks the so-called psychics on TV use in our time. But I do know her owners were using her to get rich. They were greedily exploiting her for their own gain.

Addiction. Racial prejudice. Unhealthy obsessions with sex. Violence, abuse, and neglect. Poverty. You can probably name other forces at work in this world, out to harm and destroy human life. The good news is, when we're unable to free ourselves, Jesus Christ *is* able. Sometimes our deliverance is as dramatic as the sudden freedom the Philippian slave girl experienced. At other times, freedom comes gradually, over a long time of accepting others' help and making decisive changes. Complete freedom may be found only in the next life, but Jesus' resurrection assures us of his ultimate victory over evil.

In the meantime—and it can be a mean time—evil, even though headed for defeat, isn't willing to surrender quietly. When we faithfully follow Jesus, as Paul did, we can expect to hear evil raising a ruckus along the way. Our calling is to do what we can to silence it, in our own and others' lives, in Jesus' powerful name.

Conflict with Authority

Paul's missionary journey to Philippi was bookended by conversions. Near the trip's beginning, God opened the heart of Lydia, a well-to-do Gentile businesswoman, to the gospel. She and her household were baptized, forming the nucleus of the city's Christian congregation. Near the trip's end, God opened not only another Gentile's heart but also a jail! Having seen the miraculous earthquake that broke Paul's and Silas's chains, their jailer and his household were baptized and become the newest members of the "First Church of Philippi."

Why were Paul and Silas in jail? Those greedy guys who'd just lost their fortune-telling slave girl played one of the oldest and ugliest "race cards" in history. You can hear the anti-Semitic sneer in their baseless accusation that these Jews were disturbing the peace, making trouble for Philippi's decent and upstanding citizens.

Paul and Barnabas were beaten and shackled simply for being Jewish. Few of us can identify with that specific suffering. But they were also suffering because they followed Jesus. Frankly, few who live in the United States will be able to identify with *that* specific suffering, either. Although some talk show hosts and politicians talk about supposed government attacks on Christianity, the fact is the First Amendment guarantees all Americans the right to practice their religion (or no religion at all) free from fear of imprisonment and punishment. You will not be arrested for reading this Bible study, nor will I be arrested for writing it. In the United States, Christians are not persecuted.

Unfortunately, many sisters and brothers in Christ elsewhere can't say the same. According to the Voice of the Martyrs, an organization that charts mistreatment of Christians around the world, Christians in more than forty nations today *do* face persecution: "In some of these nations it is illegal to own a Bible, to share your faith [in] Christ, change your faith or teach your children about Jesus. Those who boldly follow Christ... can face harassment, arrest, torture, and even death."[4] These Christians need our prayers; they also need us to speak out and act on their behalf.

But our own religious freedom doesn't mean our faith will never bring us into conflict with our authorities—simply because the gospel's priorities are at odds with this world's. For example, some Christians (and non-Christians working with them) in several cities have been issued citations or arrested for publicly feeding people who are homeless. City governments often point to health and safety concerns; however, those who want to distribute food frequently respond that restrictions on their activity are really ways for the "haves" to keep the "have-nots" out of sight and out of mind. Until God's new day fully dawns, faithfully following Jesus will sometimes get us into trouble—for all the right, righteous reasons.

Jesus warned his followers, "In the world you face persecution." Paul knew firsthand the truth of Jesus' words. Yet he endured conflicts with other believers, with the forces of evil, and with the world's pretenders to power because he believed Jesus' very next words: "I have conquered the world!" (John 16:33).

CHECKPOINT CHALLENGE

1. Which of these was not a hardship Paul suffered as a follower of Jesus?
   a. shipwreck
   b. going without food
   c. imprisonment
   d. danger from bandits
   e. none of the above

2. Why did Paul and Barnabas not travel together on Paul's second missionary journey?
   a. They could not agree on their itinerary.
   b. They disagreed over Paul's decision to preach to Gentiles.
   c. They disagreed about allowing John Mark to go with them.
   d. The Jerusalem church leaders did not want them to travel together, for unknown reasons.
   e. Jesus warned them in a vision that they must not travel together.

3. Who was the businesswoman who became one of the first Christians in Philippi?
   a. Priscilla
   b. Dorcas
   c. Lydia
   d. Tabitha
   e. Martha Stewart

4. What led to Paul's and Silas's arrest and imprisonment in Philippi?
   a. Paul preached about Jesus despite the town leaders' orders.
   b. Paul cast a demon out of a fortune-telling slave girl.
   c. Paul and Silas challenged pagan philosophers to a debate about the gospel.
   d. Paul and Silas were wrongfully accused of stealing from the city's treasury .

5. How were Paul and Silas freed from the Philippian prison?
   a. An earthquake broke the prisoners' chains and opened the jail's doors.
   b. The Philippian Christians staged a daring covert rescue operation.
   c. An angel of the Lord miraculously brought them out.
   d. The Philippian jailer became a believer in Christ and set them free.
   e. Scotty beamed them up.

PORTS OF CALL

Readers' Theater

Script and perform an audio drama based on Acts 16:16-40. Recruit readers to perform the roles of Paul and Silas (be sure they don't mind singing—see v. 25); the shouting, demon-possessed slave girl and her owners; and the Philippian jailer. Be sure to take advantage of this story's many opportunities for sound effects: crowds in the marketplace; beatings and flogging; jail locks and chains being shut and later broken; the waters of baptism. Be creative and dramatic. Record your performance for others in the congregation to enjoy.

After the performance, discuss these questions:

- How did Paul respond when his ministry led him into conflict?
- When, if ever, have you experienced conflict because you follow Jesus? How did you respond?

When Christians Disagree

Read Acts 15:36-41. Paul and Barnabas's disagreement over John Mark reminds us that Christians can and do, in good faith, find themselves on different sides of important issues. When we find ourselves in such a situation, remaining faithful to Jesus means also remaining faithful to each other. Paul and Barnabas went their separate ways, but each continued to serve Jesus and his church.

Identify a topic or current event about which you know Christians disagree. (If you need suggestions, ask your youth group leader or pastor.) Research some of the reasons for the disagreement. Check websites where Christians present their own view of the issue, in their own words—don't rely on attempts to put words in other people's mouths. Read the Bible texts these Christians cite in support of their position. If at all possible, talk with a Christian who has taken a position on the issue and listen to his or her arguments without, at this point, agreeing or disagreeing.

When you feel ready, write a brief summary of what you have learned, as if you are an objective news reporter. Answer these questions:

- What is the issue or topic about which Christians are disagreeing?
- What are the major points of disagreement?
- How does each side in the disagreement believe it is faithfully following Jesus?

Once you have written your objective summary, write a statement about what you believe concerning the issue and why.

A Sweet Jailbreak!

Build your own "jail cell" with graham crackers, pretzel rods, and cake frosting (your choice of flavor). Break one graham cracker sheet in half. Use dabs of frosting to stick pretzel rods (broken in half if needed) vertically on the corners and along the sides of one half of the cracker. Place the other half of the cracker on top of the pretzel rods, using more dabs of frosting to secure it in place if needed. As you look at your "cell," think and talk with others in your group about a time when faithfully following Jesus has led you, someone you know, or someone you know of into conflict or suffering. When ready, create an "earthquake" by smashing the "cell." Eat the debris, and give thanks that God is with those who suffer for following Jesus.

Praying for Persecuted Christians

Spend some time learning about Christians worldwide being persecuted for their faith. Visit such websites as the Voice of the Martyrs. Choose a particular country, and research the challenges believers there face. What practical steps can you and/or your youth ministry take to show your support for these Christians? Pray for these brothers and sisters in faith.

Speak to the Authorities

Unlike Paul, we live in a society where we are free to disagree with our authorities when we believe God calls us to do so. While Jesus doesn't expect us to pick needless fights with the powers that be, he does commission us to speak his truth about important matters. Think about a significant social issue in your community, state, or the nation that interests or concerns you. Think about such questions as:

- How does your faith in Jesus help you think about this issue?
- What Bible verses seem to connect to this issue?
- What is Jesus calling you to do about this issue?
- What is God's will for the people most affected by this issue?

After thinking and praying about these questions, write a letter to a local, state, or national elected official to let the official know why this issue matters to you as a Christian. Before you write, visit officials' websites to find out what, if anything, they have already said or done about the issue; a well-informed message will weigh more than a poorly informed one. When you write, be brief and to the point, urging specific action. You might also talk about what, if anything, your congregation or youth ministry is already doing to address the issue. Experienced social activists report that an old-fashioned, neatly handwritten letter, while less convenient than e-mail, has more impact.

Danger Ahead!

This session's study of Paul's life highlighted some of the dangers inherent in hearing and obeying God's call. Use the space below to design your own "Danger ahead!" sign. Create a sign that represents a danger or a conflict you could face or currently do face because of your commitment to Jesus.

POSTCARD PRAYER

[Leader: Have participants write responses in the "postcard" printed below, or provide actual postcards they can present in worship as an offering to God.]

Dear God, help me with your Spirit's strength when I face this conflict:

_____

_____

_____

_____

_____

Point of Departure Answer Key: a. skull and crossbones; b. a dragon and/or the words "Here there be dragons"; c. the inverted triangle "Yield" sign

Checkpoint Challenge Answer Key: 1.e; 2.c; 3.c; 4.b; 5.a

4.
CALLED TO LOVE
PAUL'S SECOND MISSIONARY JOURNEY (2)

[Love] bears all things, believes all things, hopes all things, endures all things. Love never ends.

—1 Corinthians 13:7-8

Point of Departure

Look through newspapers and magazines for advertisements that prominently feature familiar brand names or logos. Cut out a small portion of the brand or logo that could still offer someone a reasonable chance of identifying the whole. (For example, a white curve against a red background might still be recognizable as Coca-Cola's logo.)

Challenge others in your group to identify your logo, and have them challenge you to identify theirs.

Scriptures

- Acts 17:16-34
- 1 Corinthians 13

Video (Optional)

- Watch the video for *The Call*, Session 4.

GETTING OUR BEARINGS

Reading about Paul's missionary travels, we might think his world was radically different from ours. In some ways, of course, it was. Were Paul a missionary in the twenty-first century instead of the first, he'd book plane tickets on a computer and preach with PowerPoint slides. He might not be writing letters; he'd keep in constant communication with congregations via text messages and e-mails. Maybe a funny selfie snapped on the road with Silas would go viral, and the hashtag #PreacherManPaul would start trending!

But in other ways, Paul's world wasn't so different from ours. For example, think about his initial impression of Athens. Paul visited ancient Greece's most important city after stops in Thessalonica (Acts 17:1-9) and Beroea (17:10-15). He walked around this elegant, lively, culturally exciting city, renowned for its impressive architecture, its poets, and philosophers—and was shocked. Why? Because "the city was full of idols" (17:16).

Paul would likely feel the same way walking around your city, or mine. Your city isn't littered with marble statues of Greek gods and goddesses: there's no downtown temple to the god of war, Mars (aka Ares in Greek), as there was in Athens. But if we don't think today's cities are full of idols, we're either not looking hard enough, or we've gotten so used to them that they've lost their power to deeply distress us, as they did Paul.

Engaging a Culture Full of Idols

How much advertising do you see on any given day? On TV, you see about sixteen ads each day just for food and drink.[5] That number only counts straightforward commercials; it doesn't include in-show product placements, such as the *American Idol* judges' Coke glasses. You may play video games with built-in ads. (When the *Madden NFL* announcers say, "This game brought to you by Verizon," you didn't think they were simply trying for more realistic game play, did you?) Add all the advertising you scroll past or click through online: sponsored "stories" on Facebook, promoted tweets, and all those irritating pop-up windows. And don't forget to factor in ads in the real world. On billboards, in shop windows, on the clothes people wear, and the sides of the city buses they ride, you'll see images of the latest high-tech toys, the newest models of cars, the most attractive celebrities—advertising is everywhere! In

2014, total US ad spending was expected to reach just over $180 billion,[6] and every single one of those companies' dollars and cents was spent to get yours.

All these ads pitch a lot of different products, but most of them are really hawking idols. No, they don't come right out and say, "Worship something other than the one true God!" (Usually.) But as they try and persuade us to spend money on stuff they promise will make us happier, prettier, more popular, or more successful, they're tempting us, to one degree or another, to put our trust in what they're selling instead of in God. That's all an idol is: a poor substitute for God.

In ancient Athens, surrounded by idols and those who worship them, Paul could have self-righteously folded his arms across his chest, piously clucked his tongue in disapproval, and wagged a "holier-than-thou" finger in the Athenians' faces. He didn't. True to form, he first preached about Jesus in the Athenian synagogue, then took the gospel to the *agora* (AG-uh-ruh). The agora was a marketplace and so much more. An open space in which to meet and mingle, a venue for dramas and concerts, a site where you could always find stimulating philosophical discussions or heated political debate—the agora was literally and figuratively the center of city life. It was where the action was, and we know Paul well enough by now to know that he never shied away from the action! (We could say he definitely didn't suffer from ago-raphobia—the fear of open spaces—but that would just be cheesy, so let's not.)

Paul didn't avoid Athenian culture, obsessed with idols though it was. He engaged it. He met it on its own terms. He preached at Mars Hill (or the Areopagus, "hill of Ares"), within sight of the temple to the war god and all the other temples and statues that were as common in Athens as advertisements are in our culture. He complimented the Athenians for being "extremely religious" (Acts 17:22). He talked about the God he worshiped in ways they would understand, pointing out their altar to an unknown deity, and quoting their poets to illustrate his points. His sermon showed how flexible Christians can be when sharing the good news.

It also showed when Christians need to hold firm to the truth. Paul did all he could to connect his message to his audience, but he didn't do so by sacrificing its content. He couldn't pretend the Athenians should go on ignorantly groping for God, not when Jesus Christ was the One for whom they were looking, the only One who could satisfy all the longings they were trying to satisfy by worshiping idols.

When Paul got into the particulars of Jesus' death, resurrection, and future coming as judge, he lost a lot of listeners. Some believed him, but even if no one in Athens had joined the Way, Paul could have taken comfort knowing he'd been faithful to God's calling. "An obligation is laid on me," he once wrote, "and woe to me if I do not proclaim the gospel!" (1 Corinthians 9:16). Paul left Athens knowing he'd done his part to turn its people away from the empty idols and unknown gods cluttering their city and hearts. He trusted the Holy Spirit to do the rest.

Paul's Sex Talk

When it comes to idols, few are more powerful than sex. How many of those ads we talked about earlier use sex to sell something? Advertisers know sex tends to grab people's attention, and they aren't shy about exploiting it, from making suggestive wordplays to simply flashing a lot of skin.

It's no shame and no sin to be interested in sex. Most people are. And God means for us to be! God created us as sexual beings. We are physical creatures, and sex can be very physically and emotionally pleasing.

What God *didn't* intend was our society's excessive focus on sex. God gave us sex as the physical expression of an emotional and spiritual union between two people who are freely giving themselves to each other in love. The sexual union is about a lot more than two bodies coming together because it feels good. That's where sexually provocative advertising, let alone pornography, goes wrong: erotic desire is meant to be only one part of our desire to be as close to another human being as we possibly can.

The human tendency to idolize sex isn't new. When Paul reached the port city of Corinth, the last stop on his second missionary journey, he found a city that was synonymous with sexual excess. Before the Romans destroyed it in 146 B.C., it had boasted at least three temples to Aphrodite, the Greek goddess of love, and ritual sex may have been part of the worship that went on in those temples.[7] Ancient Greek-speakers felt the degree of sexual corruption in the city was so dramatic that they coined a new verb for it: "to Corinthianize."[8] In fairness, by the time Paul came along two hundred years later, Corinth wasn't exactly the same city; it had been rebuilt by Julius Caesar in 44 B.C. Still, reputations can be hard to shake, and Paul's writings to Corinth's early Christians give us reason to suspect that sex still dominated the Corinthian scene.[9]

After all, Paul said he has heard reports of "sexual immorality" within the congregation "of a kind that is not found even among pagans" (1 Corinthians 5:1). A man had been sleeping with his stepmother—and apparently no one in the church had been scandalized by this misbehavior. Why would they be? Based on what Paul goes on to say, some of the church members were still visiting prostitutes. They all seemed to have misunderstood Paul's teaching about the freedom Jesus gives. They thought that, because they believed in Jesus, they could do whatever they wanted. Their slogan was "All things are lawful for me" (6:12).

In his letter, Paul has to say a big "Yes, *but...*" to that. All things may be lawful, "but not all things are beneficial" (1 Corinthians 6:12a). He teaches the Corinthian believers that Christian freedom isn't an invitation to an ethical free-for-all, including in sexual ethics. Although he himself was unmarried (7:8), Paul understood the true significance of sex. In it, we are really joined, body and soul, to another human being—and because, as Christians, we are already joined to Jesus, we cannot take our sexual connection to others casually. As the Temple in Jerusalem was a "house of the Lord," so are the bodies of those who belong to Christ (6:15-20). Our bodies, and what we do with them, can't be separated from our spirit, or the Spirit of Christ who dwells in us.

One of the Scripture passages most commonly read at weddings is found in Paul's correspondence with the Corinthians. The words are so beautiful they're even used in marriage services that aren't specifically Christian: "Love is patient; love is kind; love is not envious or boastful or arrogant or rude" (1 Corinthians 13:4-5). We might assume Paul is describing the ideal romantic relationship, but he's not. His word for love here is *agape* (uh-GAWP-ay): an actively self-giving, even sacrificial, love, fully committed to another person's good. In ancient Greek thought, *agape* was a higher order of love than *philia* (friendship) or *eros* (erotic love), and it happened far less frequently. For Paul, *agape* love is a gift from the Holy Spirit. Whenever we see it among humans, it both flows from and points back to the only love that always lives up to Paul's description: God's self-sacrificing love for us in Jesus.

Sex in itself isn't bad. Neither are many of the other things that grab our attention. Nothing and no one but God, however, always loves us with self-sacrificial *agape*. Unlike the idols that end up weighing us down, God, with the faithful and freeing love of Jesus, lifts us up.

CHECKPOINT CHALLENGE

1. What upset Paul so much about the city of Athens?
   a. the high cost of living
   b. the presence of so many idols
   c. the lack of a synagogue in which he could preach
   d. the activity of rival Christian missionaries
   e. the suburban sprawl and traffic congestion

2. In ancient Greek cities, what was an agora?
   a. a temple dedicated to a particular god or goddess
   b. a district in which non-citizens were segregated from citizens
   c. a central place for commercial, intellectual, and cultural activity
   d. a statue of Caesar that citizens had to venerate each day

3. What is one strategy Paul does *not* use to try and connect with his audience as he preaches the gospel in Athens?
   a. He compliments them on being very religious.
   b. He tells them why their worship of idols is misguided.
   c. He quotes from poets and philosophers already familiar to them.
   d. He talks about how Jesus fulfills prophecies found in Hebrew scripture.
   e. He tells them that God has raised Jesus and appointed him as judge.

4. What answer best conveys the meaning of the ancient Greek verb "to Corinthianize"?
   a. to indulge sexual desires to excess
   b. to eat and drink too much
   c. to despise people who are poor and weak
   d. to worship Aphrodite, goddess of love, an important deity in Corinth
   e. to upholster furniture in imitation leather

5. Which of these kinds of love is, according to Paul in 1 Corinthians 13, the kind of love with which God loves us?
   a. eros
   b. philia
   c. agape

PORTS OF CALL

Outline Paul's Speech at Mars Hill

Sometimes, the best way to understand a passage of Scripture is to outline it. No, not in crayon! On a separate sheet of paper, outline Paul's speech in Acts 17:22-31 the way you would outline a speech you had to make or an essay you had to write in school. You might use the classic approach: Roman numerals indicating main points and letters indicating more specific points. You might have a system all your own that still clearly communicates the flow of Paul's thought.

Whichever format you use, don't let the paragraph breaks and verse numbers in your Bible distract you. They're not in the ancient manuscripts, and while it is true they can be helpful, they can also limit the way we look at Scripture.

- How did the process of outlining Paul's speech help you understand the way he proclaimed the gospel to the Athenians?
- Outline the way you would have continued the speech if you were Paul and had not been interrupted at the mention of Jesus' resurrection.
- Outline a simple presentation of the gospel you could make in your community (to friends at school, to neighbors, to relatives who may not believe).

Corinthian Cuisine

We can't know for certain, but perhaps Paul ate the small Greek grapes mentioned by the Roman historian Pliny around A.D. 75—"thin-skinned, juicy, and sweet.") By the sixteenth century, these small Greek grapes had come to be known as "grapes of Corinth" because Greece exported them to Europe from that port.

Find a recipe for Corinthian Raisin Cake in a cookbook or website. Prepare the recipe and let it bake as you read and do other activities in this session. (The cake can take up to forty minutes to bake.) When finished, eat some of the cake yourself and wrap up the rest to share (or, if possible, bake two). You might want to include a card with a verse from 1 Corinthians 13, to indicate that you are sharing this Corinthian cake as an expression of Christian love.

Exposing Idols

This week's Getting Our Bearings section talks about how advertisements are frequently really selling idols. It's important for us, not just as consumers but even more as Christians, to be able to recognize the ways advertising attempts to influence us. Choose a newspaper or magazine ad that grabs your attention. (Alternatively, search a video site such as YouTube for a TV ad that sticks in your memory.) Analyze the ad by answering these questions:[10]

- How easy or difficult is it to identify what product or service the ad is selling?
- How does this ad make you feel? What tone or mood does it try to create, and how?
- Describe the people you see in the ad. What are their genders, ages, ethnic backgrounds, and economic levels? What obvious or subtle messages do the people's appearances send about what the ad is selling?
- What text, if any, does the ad use? Is it used to communicate facts or to create feelings?
- Does the ad have a "plot" (is some activity taking place in the ad)? If so, what does that plot suggest about what's being sold?
- Do any symbols appear in the ad? If so, how do they reinforce the purpose of the ad?
- What values, positive or negative, does this ad directly or indirectly communicate?
- Do you think this ad could encourage people to idolize what it is selling? Why or why not?
- How do you imagine that Paul, based on your study of him so far, would react to this advertisement? What do you imagine Jesus would say?

Listening to Love Songs

A lot of popular music focuses on love, sex, and romance (not always the same things). Choose a love song (broadly defined) that you're familiar with and write down as many of its lyrics from memory as you can. Compare and contrast the song's lyrics with Paul's words about love in 1 Corinthians 13. Where do you find points of contact? Where do the song and the Scripture send different messages about the nature of love? Do you imagine Paul would recognize the love in the song as love? Why or why not?

For a creative musical challenge, try rewriting the song's lyrics to make them reflect more of 1 Corinthians 13, or try setting all or some of 1 Corinthians 13 to your own original music. Sing or recite "The Gift of Love" or some other hymn or song based on 1 Corinthians 13.

Role-Play What "Love Is"

Write each of the brief statements about love in 1 Corinthians 13:4-7 on a separate slip of scrap paper. Place all the slips in a bag or box. Have participants form small teams of two or three people. Each team draws a slip from the box and is given a few minutes to prepare a brief role play or skit presenting a situation that dramatizes or illustrates the statement about love they've selected. Encourage participants to consider love in relationships other than romantic relationships (although skits could, of course, dramatize those as well). After each skit, ask the rest of the group to talk about how the skit dramatized the statement. If possible, record the skits for others in your congregation to view.

POSTCARD PRAYER

[Leader: Have participants write responses in the "postcard" printed below, or provide actual postcards they can present in worship as an offering to God.]

Dear God, keep me focused on following you instead of these idols:

_____

_____

_____

_____

_____

Checkpoint Challenge Answer Key: 1.b; 2.c; 3.e; 4.a; 5.c

5.
CALLED TO GIVE
PAUL'S THIRD MISSIONARY JOURNEY

For you know the generous act of our Lord Jesus Christ, that though he was rich, yet for your sakes he became poor, so that by his poverty you might become rich.

—2 Corinthians 8:9

Point of Departure

Imagine you've just been given one thousand dollars "mad money"—money that is yours to do whatever you want with. Show what you'll do by filling in a pie chart on a separate sheet of paper.

Leader: For a more interactive option, have each participant cut a newspaper or magazine picture of something people can spend money on. Collect the pictures and act as an auctioneer, soliciting bids of the imaginary "mad money" on each item. Make sure participants keep track of how much money they spend.

Scriptures

- Acts 19:23-41
- 2 Corinthians 9:6-15

Video (Optional)

- Watch the video for *The Call*, Session 5.

GETTING OUR BEARINGS

One of my earliest memories of worship is of a childhood offering failure! I was sitting in a pew with Mrs. Bartley, one of those "everyone's grandmothers" who many congregations are blessed to have. One Sunday, mid-service, she nudged me and handed me a single, shiny quarter. I was excited. I immediately thought of the vending machine at our local grocery store, filled with plastic "Ancient Egyptian" trinkets I'd had my eye on for some time but that my mother never agreed to buy. Quite pleased a solution had presented itself, I pocketed the quarter and spent the rest of worship looking forward to our next trip to the store.

Sure enough, when it came, I slipped that quarter into the machine, turned the crank, and received a rinky-dink, crudely painted plastic replica of King Tut's burial mask. When my mom asked where I'd gotten the money, I told her, "Mrs. Bartley gave it to me at church!" Mom explained Mrs. Bartley had *probably* intended I drop the quarter into the offering plate. I was embarrassed. Why hadn't Mrs. Bartley just said so? Was I expected to be a mind reader?

I lost that King Tut toy a long time ago, but I've never forgotten the shame I felt about it. Mrs. Bartley had good intentions, but there are probably better ways to teach people about giving to God.

Loving Money Too Much

Encouraging Christians to give, and give generously, was a major part of Paul's ministry from its beginning. When early church leaders authorized his mission, they asked only that he "remember the poor" in Jerusalem. Paul wrote, "Which was actually what I was eager to do" (Galatians 2:10). Cynics may say Paul's eagerness to collect money was political—a little moolah to make sure he stayed in the good graces of Peter and the other apostles. But you know by now that Paul never cared too much about what others thought of him. He cared about faithfully following Christ. Although Paul likely came from a well-to-do family, he had no doubt heard stories of how Jesus, born and raised in poverty, paid special attention to people who were poor (Mark 6:34-44, for example, or Luke 6:20-26). Also, Paul preserved a saying of Jesus that we find nowhere in the four Gospels: "It is more blessed to give than to receive" (Acts 20:35). I take Paul at his word. He was eager to give because God calls God's people to give.

Of course, as my Mrs. Bartley's story demonstrates, we don't always share that eagerness!

Paul saw firsthand money's power to pull us away from God. He wrote to his protégé, the young pastor Timothy, that "the love of money" (not, as the statement is often misquoted, money itself) is "a root of all kinds of evil, and in their eagerness to be rich some have wandered away from the faith" (1 Timothy 6:10). Maybe Paul was thinking of believers in Corinth who allowed their unequal income to divide them in worship. Their celebrations of the Lord's Supper became over-the-top feasts where the rich among them gorged themselves while less fortunate members went hungry (see 1 Corinthians 11:21-22). Paul knew God calls the Christian community to live free of such status divisions. The gap between "haves" and "have-nots" is part of "the present form of this world [that] is passing away" (1 Corinthians 7:31).

Perhaps Paul also remembered how the love of money stopped some people from ever coming to faith in the first place. Ephesus (EFF-uh-sus) was a major port city on the coast of what is today southwest Turkey, and a major setting for Paul's ministry. In Acts, the apostle stayed there for more than two years, preaching and performing miracles of healing. His ministry in Ephesus proved so successful, many of the city's new Christians burned the books of magic spells on which they had depended for health and good fortune—books worth "fifty thousand silver coins" (Acts 19:19). A first-century day laborer would have had to work about 137 years to earn those wages![11] These people had invested a lot of their time and hard-earned money in magic; however, now none of that mattered, because through Paul they had encountered the true, life-changing power of the Holy Spirit.

Not everyone in Ephesus welcomed this development. One of the city's major claims to fame was the Artemision (ar-tee-MISH-un): a splendid temple honoring Artemis (Diana, in Roman mythology), goddess of the hunt and a "mother goddess" who brought fertility and health to women. This magnificent marble structure was one of the Seven Wonders of the Ancient World. It was famed for its intricately sculpted and gilded columns, the beautiful paintings on its walls, and its statue of Artemis herself, which may have stood on or even have been carved from a meteorite. (It was called "the statue that fell from heaven" in Acts 19:35.) The Artemision was not only the major religious institution in Ephesus but also a major financial one. The steady stream of worshipers who passed through its doors pumped a lot of cash into the Ephesian economy.

Just ask Demetrius. He was one of the city's many silversmiths who made a living by crafting miniature silver models of Artemis to sell to her devotees. When Demetrius saw people abandoning their magic books, he worried that the worship of Artemis couldn't compete with the worship of Christ. Demand for silver souvenirs from the temple would plummet, and Demetrius and his fellow artisans would be out of work. Convinced the Artemision was a financial institution too big to fail, Demetrius sparked a riot—"no little disturbance," Luke calls it in his wonderfully understated way (Acts 19:23). A mob got hold of two of Paul's traveling companions, Gaius and Aristarchus; it might have gotten hold of the apostle himself had not some friends held him back. The only thing that brought things back under control was the town clerk's reminder that Roman colonies must abide by Roman rules of due process or else lose their imperial privileges and protection.

It's hard to fault Demetrius for worrying about his job. But inciting mob violence? That crossed a line. On the other hand, maybe he was simply the first silversmith to speak their common fears aloud. In either case, he rejected Paul's message because it threatened his profits. Not unlike the rich ruler who let his wealth get in the way of following Jesus (Luke 18:18-23), Demetrius wouldn't embrace the gospel because he was holding too tightly to his income. Might he have been open to the message otherwise? We don't know, but we do know that he grasped—ironically, better than some Christians today seem to—the truth of Jesus' words, "You cannot serve God and wealth" (Luke 16:13). Demetrius knew the god he was serving.

God Loves Eager Givers!

While we can't serve God *and* money, we can serve God *through* money.

An often told story is about a little girl whose father gave her a dime and a dollar and let her choose which one to put in the offering plate. She gave the dime. When her crestfallen dad asked why, she said, "The preacher said God loves a cheerful giver. I decided I could feel a lot more cheerful giving the dime!"

That little girl's preacher was quoting the apostle Paul (2 Corinthians 9:7). As Paul worked to raise the funds for poor believers in Jerusalem, he discovered that some congregations were more eager to contribute to the project than others. For example, the churches in Macedonia (in Paul's day a Roman district roughly spanning what is today northern Greece) had apparently raised a remarkable amount of money given the fact they were not rolling in dough themselves (8:1-4). The Corinthian Christians were, in Paul's judgment, holding back. Where other churches were joyously giving dollars, the Corinthians were reluctantly giving dimes—if that!

Paul didn't guilt them into giving, or make wild promises about blessings they would receive if they "invested" in the collection (two tactics sometimes seen in churches today). No, Paul reminded the Corinthians that giving generously to others is the only appropriate response to what God has already so generously given in Jesus. In *The Message*, Eugene Peterson paraphrases Paul's encouragement: "You are familiar with the generosity of our Master, Jesus Christ. Rich as he was, he gave it all away for us—in one stroke he became poor and we became rich" (2 Corinthians 8:8-9).

Maybe you're fortunate, and money is no problem in your household. Maybe money is tight; it is for a lot of American families these days. Generally speaking, though, teens in the United States are pretty well-off. The average annual income of Americans twelve to fourteen years old is $2,167, and of Americans fifteen to seventeen years old is $4,023.[12] According to a 2011 poll, 33 percent of American teens spend their own money on movie tickets, 42 percent on clothing, and 51 percent on candy.[13] Teens spend about $18.50 every week.[14]

Whether you receive an allowance, pick up a regular paycheck from an after-school job, or look forward to a little "mad money" on your birthday or at Christmas, odds are you have some income you can call your own. How much of that money do you give back to God by giving it away to people in need? You won't necessarily be able to give a lot in the world's eyes (although you may be able to give more than you might assume), but, as Paul told the Corinthians, it's not the bottom line that really matters, but how eagerly you give it (2 Corinthians 8:12). God gives us material goods not only for our own needs but also, and especially, so we can play a part in "every good work" (9:8)—those same good works "God prepared beforehand to be our way of life" (Ephesians 2:10). If we hold on to money for ourselves, we're missing out on a big part of our purpose.

Paul assured the Corinthians, and us, that when we give generously, we will receive abundantly—not in terms of material blessings, but in spiritual ones. In Jesus, God has claimed us to participate in the wonderful work of sharing God's gifts with others, especially those Jesus identified as "the least" of his family (Matthew 25:40). Thanks be to God for this inexpressible gift!

CHECKPOINT CHALLENGE

1. What was wrong with the way the Christians in Corinth celebrated the Lord's Supper?
   a. They used grape juice instead of real wine.
   b. The richer members of the church overate while the poorer members went hungry.
   c. They included pagan idols in their celebrations of the Supper.
   d. They recited the wrong prayers over the bread and the cup.

2. What was the purpose of the offering Paul was collecting?
   a. To support church members in Jerusalem
   b. To support church members in Macedonia
   c. To support the first apostles of Jesus in their old age
   d. To build buildings for the new congregations he was founding

3. What was the Artemision in Ephesus?
   a. An open marketplace
   b. The seat of the ruling council of Ephesian elders
   c. A sacred scroll containing hymns that praised the goddess Artemis
   d. An elaborate temple honoring the goddess Artemis

4. Why did Demetrius incite a mob riot against Paul and his companions?
   a. Demetrius was a devout Jew who wrongly believed that Paul was preaching against observance of Torah.
   b. Demetrius believed the growing worship of Jesus would threaten his work as a maker of silver statues of Artemis.
   c. Demetrius believed Paul was preaching a foreign deity and was encouraging occult, magical practices.
   d. Demetrius thought it would make a great viral video.

5. Which of the following statements is not something Paul said to encourage Christians to give generously to others?
   a. Reminding them of Jesus' statement, "It is more blessed to give than to receive."
   b. "For the present form of this world is passing away."
   c. "Jesus Christ . . . was rich, yet for your sakes he became poor."
   d. "God loves a cheerful giver."

PORTS OF CALL

Eyewitness News from Ephesus

Working with others in your group, plan and perform a "reporter on the scene" newscast covering the "breaking news" of the riot in Ephesus, as described in Acts 19. Have reporters interview several of the people involved, such as Demetrius, Paul, rioting crowd members, and the town clerk. Make sure these interviews communicate answers to the key questions of good journalism: Who? What? Where? When? Why? How? You might also have "in-studio experts" analyze the event. Be sure to record your "newscast" so others in your congregation can see it; if your congregation has a website, investigate the possibility of posting it online.

Be a "Silversmith"

Demetrius and the Ephesian silversmiths made idols to worship. You can make a "silver" craft to remind you to worship Christ instead of idols. Using a precision knife, carefully cut a cross or other Christian symbol (a fish, a dove) from a piece of foam board (check with local craft or teacher and office supply stores). Wrap your shape in aluminum foil, making the foil over the surfaces as smooth as possible. Use a wooden stylus, pencil or ballpoint pen, or similar tool to "engrave" the foil with a pattern you design, a Bible citation, or other decoration; you could also glue on craft jewels or foam shapes for accents. Keep your craft where it will remind you to worship and serve the true God, who is not made with human hands!

What Does Your Church Give?

Many congregations make information about the church budget available to members. If your congregation does so, find out how much money your congregation receives in a year, and how much of that money is given away to "good work" (2 Corinthians 9:8) that serves those who are poor. Include not only whatever projects your congregation is directly involved with but also donations given to national and international programs, directly or through your denomination. What percentage of your congregation's income is given away? Present this information in graphic form (a bar graph or pie chart, perhaps, or a poster illustrating your congregation's giving).

- Does the amount your congregation gives surprise you? Why or why not?
- How much of your congregation's giving takes place through your youth ministry?
- How might your youth ministry raise more money for the congregation to give away?

Make a Giving Plan

Create a diagram like the one below—which you need not show to anyone else—to write a record of how much money you receive that is yours to do with as you please. Use whichever column makes the most sense for your situation: weekly, monthly, or yearly. List all sources you can think of, and estimate if you don't know exact amounts. Subtract any absolutely fixed expenses. Then identify at least one "good work" that helps those in need that you would like to support with your money, or currently support and want to support more. You might select a ministry run by your congregation, a charity operating in your community, or a national or international program to which you can donate. Write the amount you will give, choosing a timetable that makes the most sense for you. Keep this plan where you can see it as a reminder of your commitment and of your eagerness to give.

	Weekly	Monthly	Yearly
Source(s) of Income			
Good Work(s) to Support			

Plan a Love Feast

Paul reprimanded the Christians in Corinth because their celebrations of the Lord's Supper had become occasions for the well-to-do members to overindulge while "those who [had] nothing" went without (1 Corinthians 11:22). A love feast, in contrast, is a meal where all at the table have plenty to eat. John Wesley, founder of the Methodist movement, observed love feasts as "simple, ritual meal[s] in the context of which hymns are sung, Scripture is read, and testimonies and stories of faith are shared... [Love feasts] symbolize the unity of fellowship in the love of Christ which the saints at rest will share".[15]

Work with your group to plan a love feast as a part of next week's sixth and final session. Decide who will bring what. Keep the menu simple, and include plenty of bread—a reminder of Jesus, the Bread of Life (John 6:35). You might also want to include lahmacun (see Session 1) and Corinthian raisin cake (see Session 4) as edible reminders of your study of Paul. Assign responsibility for selecting one or two Scriptures to read as part of the feast, as well as one or two songs to sing or recite (you might include "Guide My Feet," with your group's additional verses from Session 2). Find someone who would be willing to speak briefly about how studying Paul has influenced their faith. Extend invitations to others from inside and outside your congregation to attend.

POSTCARD PRAYER

[Leader: Have participants write responses in the "postcard" printed below, or provide actual postcards they can present in worship as an offering to God.]

Dear God, help me commit this week to answer your call to share what I have with others in need in this way:

_____

_____

_____

_____

_____

Checkpoint Challenge Answer Key: 1.b; 2.a; 3.d; 4.b; 5.b

6.
CALLED TO BE FAITHFUL
PAUL'S DEATH AND LEGACY

*Then Paul answered, "What are you doing, weeping and breaking
my heart? For I am ready not only to be bound but even to die in
Jerusalem for the name of the Lord Jesus."*

—Acts 21:13

Point of Departure

Imagine you are writing your autobiography, many decades from now. On
a separate sheet of paper, write the title of your autobiography's last chapter
and either write the chapter's first paragraph or draw an illustration for it (or
do both!).

Scriptures

- Acts 27:13-28:10
- 2 Timothy 4:6-8

Video (Optional)

- Watch the video for *The Call*, Session 6.

GETTING OUR BEARINGS

The Bible doesn't tell us all we might like to know about the Apostle Paul.
Not once, for instance, does Scripture say what he looked like (apart from
Paul's own intriguing comment, in Galatians 6:17, that he carried "the marks

of Jesus" on his body). Late in the second century, a book that didn't make the biblical cut, The Acts of Paul and Thecla, paints this portrait: "small of stature, with a bald head and crooked legs, in a good state of body, with eyebrows meeting and nose somewhat hooked, full of friendliness."[16] So did Paul really resemble some bald-headed, bow-legged, broadly smiling ranch hand in an old cowboy movie? Maybe yes, maybe no; the Bible doesn't tell us so.

Paul's Date with Death

More intriguing, perhaps, is the fact that Scripture stays silent on the details of Paul's death. Once more, we can look to sources outside the Bible to satisfy our curiosity. In *The Call*, Adam Hamilton mentions one tradition: in Rome, the Church of the Three Fountains marks the spot where, legend has it, Paul's freshly cut-off head fell to the ground and bounced three times, causing a spring of water to bubble up from each point of impact! That's pretty gross *and* pretty cool—but you won't find it in the Bible.

You won't find *anything* about Paul's death in Scripture except the fact that he was fully prepared to die as a result of his commitment to Christ. When he says a tearful good-bye to church leaders in Ephesus, he tells them he is determined to go to Jerusalem—even as Jesus "set his face to go to Jerusalem" to die (Luke 9:51)—"not knowing what will happen" there, knowing only that the Spirit has told him that "in every city...imprisonment and persecutions are waiting" (Acts 20:22-23). As it turned out, Paul didn't die in Jerusalem as Jesus did; however, he was arrested and beaten there on the basis of questionable charges, as Jesus was (21:27-36). And from Jerusalem, Paul set out on a journey that eventually took him to Rome, where tradition holds he was executed as part of the Emperor Nero's sadistic persecution of Christians.

The Roman historian Tacitus offers a gripping account of how Nero, eager to find a scapegoat for a massive fire that destroyed much of the city in A.D. 64, punished followers of the Way:

> [F]irst those were seized who admitted their faith, and then, using the information they provided, a vast multitude were convicted....They were killed by dogs by having the hides of beasts attached to them, or they were nailed to crosses or set aflame, and, when the daylight passed away, they were used as nighttime lamps.[17]

Tactius's history makes us think that if Paul actually was beheaded, he was lucky in a grim sort of way—it would've been a quicker death.

But Paul was not afraid to die for following Jesus. As he knew his death drew near, he wrote to his protégé Timothy, "I have fought the good fight, I have finished the race, I have kept the faith" (2 Timothy 4:7). These aren't the words of someone looking back on his life with regret. Paul knew he had successfully completed the work God gave him to do. As physical athletes in the ancient world won laurel crowns celebrating their victories, Paul, a spiritual athlete, looked forward to receiving the "crown of righteousness" (4:8)—his full and final entrance into an eternal relationship with God. Why should Paul fear death when that sort of life awaited him?

You and I may never have to choose between professing our faith and saving our skins. You may, however, face situations in which it would be easier to downplay or ignore your Christian identity. Maybe your school's popular kids think going to church is a lame waste of a perfectly good Sunday morning. Maybe you know mentioning your faith at team practice or your after-school job will only invite others to mock you. Maybe you're worried that writing too passionately about church involvement in a college application essay will hurt your chances of getting an acceptance letter in return. Such situations are challenging. No one can tell you what to do. But remember Paul, who refused to stop hoping in the promises of God (Acts 26:6-7), even when going "all in" on God's promises meant he was going to his death.

One Last Adventure

The original readers of Acts, of course, already knew Paul's fate. That fact may explain why Luke doesn't dwell on the apostle's last days. He'd rather his readers remember Paul in his prime. And so he ends his book with Paul under house arrest in Rome but still alive, "proclaiming the Kingdom of God and teaching about the Lord Jesus Christ with all boldness and without hindrance" (Acts 28:31). What a great final image! The Roman authorities can shut Paul away—but they can't shut him up. As Paul once wrote to Timothy, he may have been "chained like a criminal," but "the word of God is not chained" (2 Timothy 2:9).

But Luke leaves readers with more than memories of Paul the preacher. In his account of Paul's tumultuous trip to Rome—a harrowing sea journey that, based on the reappearance of the pronoun "we" in Acts 27-28, Luke himself may have shared—Luke essentially revisits some of the "greatest hits" of Paul's ministry. Under the guidance of the Spirit, he highlights certain events in order to remind readers that God was no less present with and active through Paul near the end of Paul's life than God had been during the rest of it.

The story of Paul's shipwreck and stay on Malta (an island sixty miles south of Sicily) echoes some earlier episodes from Paul's missionary travels. When, for example, Paul confounded all expectations by surviving a snakebite, the natives of Malta began to wonder whether he was a god— the same mistake some people in Lystra made about him and Barnabas (Acts 14:8-18). And when we read about Paul miraculously healing so many of the island's sick, we can hardly help but remember how God's healing power flowed even through Paul's handkerchiefs in Ephesus (19:11-12), or how Paul healed the girl who was possessed by a future-telling demon and exploited by her owners in Philippi.

As a castaway on Malta, Paul seemed part Ulysses, part Indiana Jones, part Superman. Mostly, though, he was reminiscent of Jesus. He spoke of mercy for the captives, as Jesus spoke (see Luke 4:18). He overcame what should have been the deadly strike of a literal serpent, as Jesus overcame the deadly strike of the figurative serpent Satan (an ancient Christian interpretation of Genesis 3:15; see also Revelation 20:2). Paul healed the sick, as Jesus healed.

Luke's record of this unexpected "bonus" missionary journey to Malta wouldn't have made the original readers of Acts forget about how Paul had died, but it would have made them think more about how Paul had lived: in the power and the spirit of Jesus Christ. Reading about those events may have motivated readers to live that way themselves. When they did, Jesus would have worked through them and been seen in them, just as he had worked through Paul and been seen in Paul. Readers may even have remembered Paul's words, "Be imitators of me, as I am of Christ" (1 Corinthians 11:1).

Called to Proclaim Christ

Some readers of Paul criticize him for that instruction. They claim it reveals his arrogance. What gives Paul the right, they ask, to hold himself up as a role model like that? Here's one more smug and self-satisfied Christian, insisting everyone else be just like him.

Paul wasn't without his faults. He could be rash; he could be bullheaded; being human, he had it in him to be arrogant. But he never insisted that everyone else be just like him. He *did* insist that all Christians be like Christ. He wanted the Corinthians, and other believers, to imitate him only to the extent that he imitated Jesus. At his hearing before King Agrippa, Paul said he prayed that all who heard him might be like him, except for his chains (Acts 26:29). Paul wanted Christians to trust and pin their ultimate hopes on the promises of God, promises of new life and salvation, in this world and the next, that had been fulfilled in Jesus.

Frankly, Paul might be surprised to learn his writings had been added to the Scripture he knew and amazed that so many Christians study the story of his life and ministry so closely. I don't doubt he'd also be pleased—but not because he ever thought he was the main attraction. "Was Paul crucified for you?" he once sarcastically asked the Corinthians (1 Corinthians 1:13). Paul fearlessly taught and lived his faith because he knew that, in a sense, he'd already died: "I have been crucified with Christ; and it is no longer I who live, but it is Christ who lives in me" (Galatians 2:19b-20). Paul never hesitated to tell his story, but only spoke about himself to point others to God. "By the grace of God I am what I am," Paul wrote, "and his grace toward me has not been in vain" (1 Corinthians 15:10).

You may not remember everything we've covered in these six sessions, but remember this: the same God, revealed in the risen and living Jesus Christ and who showed amazing grace to Paul, also shows amazing grace to you and calls you to tell your story—not just in speech, but in actions—so that other people might realize the grace God shows them too. What you say and do today may end up mattering to someone in your life even more than what Paul said and did two thousand years ago. God may use those words and deeds to show others the truth that God's love in Jesus is more powerful than anything else in all creation, even death; and that nothing can separate us from that love (Romans 8:37-39).

Proclaiming and putting that good news, that best of all possible news, into practice is the call all believers receive from "God our Savior, who desires everyone to be saved and to come to the knowledge of the truth" (1 Timothy 2:3-4). How will you answer?

CHECKPOINT CHALLENGE

1. Based on what we know from Acts, which of these statements accurately describes Paul's death?
   a. He died in Jerusalem, like Jesus.
   b. He died in Rome during the Emperor Nero's persecution of Christians.
   c. He was prepared to face death as a consequence of following Jesus.
   d. He was beheaded.

2. In his testimony to King Agrippa, Paul said he was on trial for what reason?
   a. Because he had been accused of telling people to disobey the emperor
   b. Because of his hope in God's promises to Israel
   c. Because of his former behavior as a persecutor of Christians
   d. Because certain Jewish leaders were jealous of his successful preaching

3. On what island was Paul shipwrecked as he sailed to Rome?
   a. Crete
   b. Sicily
   c. Cyprus
   d. The Island of Misfit Toys
   e. Malta

4. Which of the following things did not happen during that shipwreck and its aftermath?
   a. Paul predicted that no one aboard the ship would die.
   b. Paul survived a potentially deadly snakebite.
   c. Paul healed many sick people on the island.
   d. Paul established a congregation to which he later wrote letters.

5. How does Luke end his account of Paul's life in Acts?
   a. Paul writes a final, farewell letter to the congregations he helped establish.
   b. Paul, under house arrest in Rome, is still preaching and teaching about Jesus.
   c. Paul, alone in a Roman jail cell, prays that God will strengthen him to face his death.
   d. Paul is preparing to deliver his defense before the emperor himself.

PORTS OF CALL

Boat Races

Challenge your friends to a boat-building and boat-racing contest. Find directions online for folding paper boats. Construct your boats; decorate them if you wish. Place the finished boats in one end of a shallow tub of water and blow on them—gently at first, like the "moderate south wind" the sailors first enjoyed (Acts 27:13)—to see whose boat reaches the other end first. For a follow-up race, blow harder—like the violent northeaster that "rushed down from Crete" (27:14)—and see whose boat survives the longest. (For a really powerful wind, use an electric fan!) After the races (and likely after all the boats have been swamped), discuss these questions:

- Paul received assurance of God's protecting presence through an angel (27:23-24). How do you experience the assurance of God's presence?
- Talk about a frightening situation in which your faith in God has encouraged you or others, as Paul's faith did.

Sing a Song

Sing or recite "Lonely the Boat," "Stand By Me," or some other hymn or song that uses storm imagery to celebrate God's protection and guidance through difficult and frightening times.

Spiritual Sports Headlines

Read 2 Timothy 4:6-8. Paul is using imagery from ancient sports—wrestling and racing—to describe his endurance and victory as a follower of Jesus. Try paraphrasing Paul with images drawn from modern sports. How might he make the same point to NFL fans, for example, or to avid followers of World Cup soccer? Combine your responses with others' and publish a "sports page" or produce a "sportscast" that communicates these verses' message in modern terms. Think and talk about this question: How do you want people to remember your Christian faith when you have finished your race?

Paul's Letter to Your Church

Consider what you know about Paul after these six sessions.
- What are your strongest impressions of Paul?

- Have your opinions of Paul changed during this study? If so, how?
- What do you still want to know about Paul? How will you find out?

Now imagine that Paul is writing a letter to your congregation (or even specifically to your youth ministry). What would he want to say? In most (though not all) of Paul's letters, he usually has both praise and criticism for the believers looking to him for guidance. What does your congregation do that Paul would applaud? What might he have concerns about? What specific advice would he give your congregation on reaching out to its local community with the gospel? If you'd like your "letter" to be in a modern format, record a video message from the apostle. Show your finished product to your congregational leaders and discuss it with them. What do they think about your ideas of what Paul would have to say? How can you and your youth ministry work together with the leadership to address the issues raised in your "letter from Paul"?

POSTCARD PRAYER

[Leader: Have participants write responses in the "postcard" printed below, or provide actual postcards they can present in worship as an offering to God.]

Dear God, help me follow the example of your apostle Paul in this specific way:

_____

_____

_____

_____

_____

Checkpoint Challenge Answer Key: 1.c; 2.b; 3.e; 4.d; 5.b

Notes

1. See Morna D. Hooker, "The Letter to the Philippians," *New Interpreter's Bible* (Nashville: Abingdon Press, 2000), vol. 11, p. 526.

2. Libby Copeland, "No escape: The long vacation is a thing of the past," *Crain's Chicago Business*, July 21, 2012; accessed January 22, 2015. http://www .chicagobusiness.com/article/20120721/ISSUE03/307219986/no-escape -the-long-vacation-is-a-thing-of-the-past,.

3. Public Policy Polling, "Halloween Viewed Favorably by Most Americans," October 30, 2012; http://www.publicpolicypolling.com/pdf/2011 /HalloweenRelease%2BResults.pdf, Question 13.

4. "Persecution Worldwide," http://www.prisoneralert.com/vompw_persecution .htm; accessed February 3, 2015.

5. Common Sense Media Research, "Advertising to Children and Teens: Current Practices," Spring 2014; https://www.commonsensemedia.org/research /advertising-to-children-and-teens-current-practices, 7.

6. "Total US Ad Spending to See Largest Increase Since 2004," http://www .emarketer.com/Article/Total-US-Ad-Spending-See-Largest-Increase-Since -2004/1010982#sthash.K7kfkaOa.dpuf.

7. Corinth: Aphrodite of Cities," *In the Footsteps of Paul*, PBS, 2003; http://www .pbs.org/empires/peterandpaul/footsteps/footsteps_6_2.html.

8. D. A. Carson and Douglas J. Moo, *An Introduction to the New Testament* (Grand Rapids: Zondervan, 2009), 420.

9. See J. Paul Sampley, "The First Letter to the Corinthians," *The New Interpreter's Bible* (Nashville: Abingdon Press, 2002), vol. 10, p. 775.

10. Some questions adapted from Arthur Asa Berger, "How to Analyze an Advertisement," Center for Media Literacy; http://www.medialit.org /reading-room/how-analyze-advertisement#bio.

11. See Robert W. Wall, "The Book of Acts," *The New Interpreter's Bible* (Nashville: Abingdon Press, 2002), vol. 10, p. 269.

12. http://www.statisticbrain.com/teenage-consumer-spending-statistics/.

13. "$211 Billion and So Much to Buy—American Youths, the New Big Spenders," Harris Interactive, October 25, 2011; http://www.harrisinteractive.com /NewsRoom/PressReleases/tabid/446/ctl/ReadCustom%20Default/mid /1506/ArticleId/896/Default.aspx.

14. Joyce Kauf, "Teen Time," *Rapaport Magazine*, June 2013; http://www.diamonds .net/Magazine/Article.aspx?ArticleID=43311&RDRIssueID=111.

15. "What is an Agape Meal?," http://www.umc.org/what-we-believe/what-is-an -agape-meal.

16. Quoted by James Tabor, "The Quest for the Historical Paul," *Bible History Daily*, August 14, 2014; http://www.biblicalarchaeology.org/daily/people-cultures-in- the-bible/people-in-the-bible/the-quest-for-the-historical-paul/.

17. Quoted in *Reading About the World*, vol. 1, Paul Brians et al., eds., 3rd ed. (Harcourt Brace Custom Books, 1999) http://public.wsu.edu/~brians /world_civ/worldcivreader/world_civ_reader_1/tacitus.html.

CPSIA information can be obtained at www.ICGtesting.com
Printed in the USA
LVOW10s2354160915

454164LV00007BA/23/P

9 781630 882686